THE SPANISH SUCCESSION WAR.

— — — — — — —

.

.

.

By

August Friedrich Wilhelm E d l e

b.A.,1906.

.

Washington, D.C.

1 9 0 7.

I N D E X.

-   I   -

Bibliography.
_____

Ernest Lavisse et Alfred Rambaud, Histoire générale du IVe siècle
    à nos jours. Tome XIV, Louis XIV.

Coxe, Memoirs of the kings of Spain of the house of Bourbon, from
    the access of Philippe V.

Gaedecke, Die Politik Oesterreichs in der spanischen Erbfolgefrage

Noorden, Der spanische Erbfolgekrieg.

Landau, Geschichte Karls VI als König von Spanien

Targe, Histoire de l´avènement de la maison de Bourbon au trône
    d´Espagne.

Henri Martin, History of France from the most remote period
    to 1789.

-   -   -   -   -   -   -   -   -   -   -

T H E   F I R S T   PARTITION   T R E A T Y.

Charles II, king of Spain, at the age of 18 years, had married in 1679 Mary Louisa, daughter of Philip, duke of Orleans. Ten years later Mary Louisa died, and in 1690 Charles took as a second wife Mary Anne, daughter of Philip William, Count Palatine of Neuburgh. As both marriages had been without issue, and Charles, suffering from a lingering and hopeless malady, was not predicted a long life, the question of the inheritance of the Spanish throne agitated more or less all the cabinets of Europe.

Spain, though at this period in a most deplorable state of weakness, which was especially true of her army and navy, was still, if not one of the most powerful, yet one of the largest empires of the world. It comprised

1) in Europe the kingdoms of Castille, Aragon and Navarra, further Milan, Naples, Sicily, Sardine, Toscana and the marquisdom of Finale on the bay of Genoa,

2) fortified places in Africa (Ceuta, Mellila)

3) African islands (the Canaries),

4) the Philippine and Caroline islands,

5) the islands of Cuba, Porto Rico, Trinidad,

6) in America: Florida with the neighboring islands, Mexico (with
   Texas), California, all Central America and the whole of
   South America, except Brazil.

There was quite a number of claimants for the succession, the
Dauphin, Emperor Leopold, the electoral prince of Bavaria,Philip,
duke of Orleans, and Victor Amadeus, duke of Savoy.

The Dauphin claimed succession to the Spanish throne as son
of Maria Theresa (wife of Louis XIV), the oldest daughter of
Philip IV of Spain, and also as grandson of Anne (wife of Louis
XIII), daughter of Philip III of Spain, in spite of the fact,that
his mother as well as his grandmother had renounced all claims
to the succession, and that this renunciation had been confirmed
by the king, and granted ratification by the law giving body in
Spain, the Cortes, whereby it gained validity. Still Maria
Theresa's dowry had not been paid in time, and upon this circum-
stance Louis XIV based his claims for the Dauphin, declaring the
renunciation valid.

Emperor Leopold, as descendant from Philip, archduke of Austria
and Johanna of Castile, on one hand, and as son of Mary Anne,
daughter of Philip III, on the other, pretended to be entitled to

inherit the throne of Spain. In order to avoid the jealousy of
the other great powers of Europe, which would greatly disapprove
the union of the large empires of Spain and Austria under one
sovereign, Leopold as well as his oldest son Joseph gave up their
rights in favor of Charles, the second son of Leopold.

Joseph Ferdinand, electoral prince of Bavaria, founded his
pretensions upon the rights of his grandmother, Margaret Therese
(first wife of Emperor Leopold I), daughter of Philip IV of
Spain. Margaret too, when marrying Leopold, had relinquished her
rights to the Spanish throne, but this renunciation was neither
confirmed by king Philip IV, nor ratified by the Cortes. Thus
Joesph Ferdinand might have been considered the legitimate heir
of Charles II.

Philip, duke of Orleans, brother of Louis XIV, claimed his
rights from Anne, daughter of Philip III of Spain, who, as already
mentioned, had renounced her rights.

Victor Amadeus, duke of Savoy, derived his claims from his
great grandmother Catherine, second daughter of Philip II of
Spain.

The pretensions of the dukes of Orleans and Savoy, however, did
not come into consideration at all, due probably more to the in-
feriority of the candidates' position than to that of their claims

In France, ever since the marriage of Louis XIV with Maria

Theresa, the opinion had been spread out that the renunciation
of the queen would not cut short the rights of her children as the
law of succession could not be changed by it.

The greatest anxiety was felt by the different parties to pur-
sue their interests at the court in Madrid. There were two
German parties according to the two candidates: One, to which
the queen mother belonged, considered the rights of the prince
elector Joseph Ferdinand of Bavaria prior to those of Emperor
Leopold or his son Charles. It was supported by some members of
the cabinet, and by count of Oropesa, retired, who was, however,
frequently consulted by the king. The second, having in view
the interests of archduke Charles, consisted of the present queen
(formerly an Austrian princess), and of cardinal Portocarero and
the majority of the cabinet.

The king himself seemed to favor the claims of the Bavarian
prince, but very sick and of a weak character, could easily be
influenced.

The Austrian side was furthermore well represented at the court
by Ferdinand Bonaventuro count of Harrach, Emperor Leopold's
able ambassador. The latter succeeded in considerably increas-
ing the sympathy for archduke Charles, and even obtained the promise of the king to nominate the archduke his successor. Charles'
only condition was that emperor Leopold should send the archduke

to Madrid together with an army of 10 000 men, because he appreh-
ended troubles with France. Strange enough, Leopold did not profit of this success gained by his ambassador, as he sent neither
the archduke nor the army to Spain. It may be presumed that this
failure was due to the weak financial conditions of the Emperor,
fear of France, or apprehension that the archduke's life would
be in danger in Madrid in such a critical situation.

The influence of the house of Bourbon at the Spanish court was
small about this time, and it owed the little there was, more to
an aversion, those persons entertained for Germany than to their
sympathy for France. But Louis XIV had watched anxiously every-
thing occuring in Spain. Already before this time he had tried
to conciliate gradually the Spanish king and people, in giving
back to Spain,(by the peace of Ryswick), all the conquests he had
made from it. Seeing the Austrian influence growing more and more
in Madrid he sent as his ambassador the marquis (later duke) of
Harcourt, a very clever diplomat, to look after his interests.
Harcourt, by the splendor and lavishness he displayed, and his
fine social qualities, soon won the hearts of the Spaniards for
himself and his osvereign's cause.

In the degree the French influence grew, the Austrian began to
decrease, and after even the cardinal of Portocarrero had relinquished the Austrian cause, Harrach requested his recall, and

was replaced by his son Louis, who possessed neither the talents
of his father nor any diplomatic experience, and was therefore of
little avail. At the same time Louis XIV had not been idle. His
army was not dismissde after the peace of Rysmick, but had, on the
contrary, been gradually increased at theSpanish frontier, and the
French harbors were filled with men of war. These measures were
apparently taken to prevent emperor Leopold from any decisive
actions. Louis XIV was also active in another direction, which
made him appear very disinterested as to the Spanish affairs, ex-
cluded the Austrian prince from the succession of the throne
Charles´ II, and served admirably his plans in Madrid. He negotiat
ed with the two seapowers, England and Holland, pretending that
he had no interest in the Dauphin ever ascending the Spanish
throne, and that he was willing to abandon that scheme, in order
to preserve peace. These negotiations led, in 1698, to the so
called First Partition Treaty between France and the two maritime powers. The partition was to be made after Charles´ II
death as follows:

Spain and the Indies, with the Netherlands, were to fall to the
electoral prince of bavaria; Milan to the archduke Charles;
Naples and Sicily with the marquisate of Finale to the Dauphin.
In case the electoral prince should happen to die after the

was replaced by his son Louis, who possessed neither the talents
of his father nor any diplomatic experience, and was therefore of
little avail. At the same time Louis XIV had not been idle. His
army was not dismissde after the peace of Rysnick, but had, on the
contrary, been gradually increased at theSpanish frontier, and the
French harbors were filled with men of war. These measures were
apparently taken to prevent emperor Leopold from any decisive
actions. Louis XIV was also active in another direction, which
made him appear very disinterested as to the Spanish affairs, ex-
cluded the Austrian prince from the succession of the throne
Charles' II, and served admirably his plans in Madrid. He negotiat
ed with the two seapowers, England and Holland, pretending that
he had no interest in the Dauphin ever ascending the Spanish
throne, and that he was willing to abandon that scheme, in order
to preserve peace. These negotiations led, in 1698, to the so
called First Partition Treaty between France and the two maritime powers. The partition was to be made after Charles' II
death as follows:

Spain and the Indies, with the Netherlands, were to fall to the
electoral prince of Bavaria; Milan to the archduke Charles;
Naples and Sicily with the marquisate of Finale to the Dauphin.
In case the electoral prince should happen to die after the

accession, without leaving descendants, his father was to inherit
the crown of Spain.   Austria and bavaria not consenting to this
partition, were to be attacked by the united forces of the three
powers which, if victorious, would decide afterwards to whom the
respective portions were to fall.

From this treaty France derived considerable advantages.   In
the first place is was going to separate Austria from the maritime
powers, and make opponents of Austria and Bavaria, thus leaving
France more or less free hand regarding Spain.   Then there was
little doubt that if the bavarian prince was really to ascend the
Spanish throne, France would be awarded the Netherlands for her
generosity.   Furthermore as the maritime powers were secretly pointed out to Charles II as the authors of the plan, Spain and her
king would highly resent their action, their influence consequently decrease, and that of France grow.   But above all it would keep
Charles II from nominating the Austrian archduke his successor,
because the succession would mean certain war with the three great
powers which made the treaty, as it was clearly shown by the
latter that they did not want an Austrian prince on the Spanish
throne.

How well Louis XIV had calculated was soon shown by the result
of the partition treaty.   Chalres II made a will by which the
rights of the Bavarian prince were approved, and he therefore

nominated as successor of Charles II on the Spanish throne.
This will meant the triumph of the French diplomacy over the
Austrian, which was completely defeated in Spain.

- - - - -

THE SECOND PARTITION TREATY.

The will of Charles II of Spain, nominating as his successor the Bavarian prince was brought officially to the cognizance of Louis XIV. He made a formal protest, stating that he consented only in so far as the rights of the French line were not interfered with.

Scarcely was this measure taken, when the death of the prince of Bavaria occured, thus frustrating the testament of the king of Spain. As chief pretendants were only left now the Bourbon and the Austrian candidates, and the intrigues, scarcely discontinued, were started again by the two courts. But Louis XIV was not only active in Spain, he succeeded in arranging a Second Partition Treaty with England and Holland, the terms of which were the following:

Spain, the Netherlands and the Indies to be reserved for Archduke Charles, who would be considered universal heir.

The Dauphin to renounce his rights regarding the Spanish crown, and to receive Naples and Sicily instead.

The Emperor and his oldest son to declare solemnly that they ceded their pretensions for the Spanish succession to the Archduke

The Emperor to give his consent to this treaty within three months, and the Archduke not to be allowed to enter Spain or the Italian dominions until after the death of Charles. If he was going to try to do so while Charles was still living, the three powers considered themselves entitled to prevent it by force.

By the second partition treaty France became virtually master of the situation, eliminating almost perfectly the Austrian candidacy in excluding the archduke from Spain until after the death of the king. Louis, under the pretext of carrying out the directions of the treaty, was enabled to increase his military and naval forces at the Spanish frontier.

The Emperor, however, was not satisfied with the stipulations of the treaty — he wanted the whole, not a part of it. Thus he allowed the three months to pass without announcing his consent.

Meanwhile the French agents, especially Portocarrero and the French ambassador were busy in Madrid to declare William and the United Provinces to be the authors of the second partition treaty who, they said, were only joined by Louis XIV for fear the rights of the Bourbon line might be passed over. In this way the resentment of Charles was directed towards England and Holland while the influence of France grew correspondingly. They caused also an overestimation of France's power in Spain, while Austria,

separated from the sea powers was set forth as absolutely power-
less. At the same time they took care that the public opinion
was by-and-by persuaded of the validity of the Dauphin s rights.

The chief arguments brought forth by the Bourbon partisans for
the bourbon succession was, that the renunciation of their rights
were only asked from the infantas to avoid the union of the crowns
of France and Spain upon one head. The guaranty was given now
that this would not be the case, the renunciation thereby becoming
void. The Austrian party responded, "that the king of France had
bound himself by the most solemn engagements to dismember the
succession; that he had expressed his resolution to accept no will
in favor of his family; and consequently that the indivisibility
of the monarchy rested solely on the House of Austria."

These representations, emphasized especially by the queen and
Oropesa, impressed the poor monarch deeply, as he was naturally
attached to his family, and he gave the Emperor assurances that
the archduke would be nominated universal heir.

The French party succeeded, however, in making Charles waver
in this resolution, and in his mental agony he decided, upon the
advice of Portocarrero, to consult the pope. The result could
not be doubtful, as Innocent XII, jealous of the house of Austria,
would not think of recommending the archduke for the Spanish
succession. Innocent's answer justified the expectations of the

bourbon party. He replied that Charles was bound in conscience to nominate one of the younger sons of the Dauphin, either the duke of Anjou or the duke of Berri, provided that precautions were take to prevent the union of the two crowns. Still Charles was hesitating to disinherit his family, and asked the opinion of the Council of Castile as well as of the Council of the State, and only after both (led by Portocarrero) had spoken in favor of the Bourbons, he made his will and named the duke of Anjou his successor.

Charles II, the last male representative of the Austrian dynasty in Spain, died on the 3rd of November 1700, and duke Philip of Anjou, second son of the Dauphin, was proclaimed king of Spain under the name of Philip V immediately after the opening of Charles testament.

-   -   -   -   -   -   -

OPEN HOSTILITIES.

It was another victory of the French diplomacy over the Austrian that Charles II had nominated Philip, duke of Anjou, his successor, causing at the courts of London and at the Hague anxiety and alarm, at the court of Vienna the greatest resentment. There was general rejoicing in Paris at the beginning, but soon it became a certainty that the accession of Philip V in Spain meant war not only with the Emperor but also with England and Holland with which countries Louis XIV had concluded the two treaties of partition. Louis, however, placed the glory and profit of his family above the welfare of France, and was only too glad to accept the appointment of his grandson. Still, in order to justify his conduct to some degree, and not to make it too evident that he had been playing an underhand game with the maritime powers, he made up the following political farce:
He refused to receive the ambassador who was sent from Spain with the will, until the matter would have been considered by the Council. The result of the deliberation of this body was, as nobody had doubted, the advice that Louis XIV should accept the

will of the late king of Spain, and allow Philip of Anjou to
leave France for Spain in order to accede to the throne of that
country.

Louis accepted thereupon formally the will, and summoning the
Dauphin and his children, the dukes of Burgundy, Anjou and Berri,
as well as the Spanish ambassador to his room, addressed Philip
of Anjou in this way:

"Sir, the king of Spain has made you a king. The nobles demand
you, the people desire you, and I give my consent. You are going
to reign over the greatest monarchy in the world, and over a
brave people who have been ever distinguished for their honor and
loyalty. I recommend you to love them, and gain their affection
by the mildness of your government."

On the 4th of January, 1701, the young king of Spain left Paris
On this occasion Louis XIV said memorable words to Philip, point-
ing at the Royal princes, - words which revealed his real politics
and which showed what Europe might expect from the accession of
the Bourbons to the Spanish throne:

" behold the princes of my blood and of yours. The two nations
must consider themselves but as one; they ought to have the same
interests; and therefore I hope that these princes will be as muc'
attached to you as to me. Henceforth there will be no Pyrenees."-

Soon the news arrived in France that her enemies intended to

will of the late king of Spain, and allow Philip of Anjou to
leave France for Spain in order to accede to the throne of that
country.

Louis accepted thereupon formally the will, and summoning the
Dauphin and his children, the dukes of Burgundy, Anjou and Berri,
as well as the Spanish ambassador to his room, addressed Philip
of Anjou in this way:

"Sir, the king of Spain has made you a king. The nobles demand
you, the people desire you, and I give my consent. You are going
to reign over the greatest monarchy in the world, and over a
brave people who have been ever distinguished for their honor and
loyalty. I recommend you to love them, and gain their affection
by the mildness of your government."

On the 4th of January, 1701, the young king of Spain left Paris
On this occasion Louis XIV said memorable words to Philip, point-
ing at the Royal princes, — words which revealed his real politics
and which showed what Europe might expect from the accession of
the Bourbons to the Spanish throne:

" Behold the princes of my blood and of yours. The two nations
must consider themselves but as one; they ought to have the same
interests; and therefore I hope that these princes will be as much
attached to you as to me. Henceforth there will be no Pyrenees.".

Soon the news arrived in France that her enemies intended to

contest the heritage gained by the Bourbons through undue means.

Louis took now into consideration to win allies for the approaching struggle. The first to join him was the gallant elector of Bavaria, Max Emannuel. Between the Emperor and the bavarian ruler existed animosity since the time the late king of Spain had appointed the young Bavarian prince Ferdinand Joseph his heir. Though the poor prince was dead, the hostility between the two monarchs had not ceased, and it was therefore natural that the elector made common cause with Louis. The king of France promised him for his assistance the Spanish Netherlands and the Palatinate. The possession of those Austrian territories which he might still occupy at the end of the war, was also guaranteed to him.

Another ally of France was the brother of the elector of Bavaria, Joseph Clemens, Archbishop of Cologne. As Louis XIV had once used all his influence to have the bishop of Strassburg nominated archbishop of Cologne, while the Emperor succeeded in securing this place for the young Bavarian prince Joseph Clemens, the attitude of the archbishop towards the Emperor now meant an act of ingratitude and unloyalty.

Victor Amadeus, duke of Savoy, was won by Louis when Philip V of Spain solicited the duke's daughter in marriage.

Emperor Leopold I had also lost no time in finding adherents for his cause. At his instigation the so-called Great Alliance

contest the heritage gained by the Bourbons through undue means.

Louis took now into consideration to win allies for the approaching struggle. The first to join him was the gallant elector of Bavaria, Max Emannuel. Between the Emperor and the bavarian ruler existed animosity since the time the late king of Spain had appointed the young Bavarian prince Ferdinand Joseph his heir. Though the poor prince was dead, the hostility between the two monarchs had not ceased, and it was therefore natural that the elector made common cause with Louis. The king of France promised him for his assistance the Spanish Netherlands and the Palatinate. The possession of those Austrian territories which he might still occupy at the end of the war, was also guaranteed to him.

Another ally of France was the brother of the elector of Bavaria, Joseph Clemens, Archbishop of Cologne. As Louis XIV had once used all his influence to have the bishop of Strassburg nominated archbishop of Cologne, while the Emperor succeeded in securing this place for the young Bavarian prince Joseph Clemens, the attitude of the archbishop towards the Emperor now meant an act of ingratitude and unloyalty.

Victor Amadeus, duke of Savoy, was won by Louis when Philip V of Spain solicited the duke's daughter in marriage.

Emperor Leopold I had also lost no time in finding adherents for his cause. At his instigation the so-called Great Alliance

was formed at the Hague, on the 7th of September, 1701, between him
and the sea powers, England and Holland. The Emperor had to con-
tend himself with the promise of his allies to assist him in con-
quering the Italian dependencies of the Spanish crown. This re-
striction of the obligations of the members of the alliance was
the work of William III of England who thought the peace of
Europe endangered to the same degree if Spain would wholly come
in the Emperor´s possession as by the union of the French and
Spanish crowns.

In the beginning Willia. found great resistance in the parliament with regard to the war, but soon an event occured that changed
the situation completely. This was the death of king James II,
the Stuart, who, expelled from England, had found a refuge with
Louis XV. His son assumed the name of king James III of England
and the king of France recognised his pretensions to the English
throne. This caused indignation in England to such a degree that
the parliament granted immediately the means demanded by William
for the war against France. It now asked   him not to grant
peace to Louis until the English nation had been given sufficient
satisfaction for the insult.

The alliance formed by the Emperor was also entered by Hanover
and Brandenburg - Prussia. As reward the duke of Hanover was
made elector, the elector of Brandeburg, Frederick III, king.

17

Frederick had long had the desire, not from vanity, but from the just appreciation of the strong position of his electorate in the empire, to be nominated king. Still, according to the constitution of the empire every promotion in rank had to be granted by the emperor, and the latter had not been inclined to raise Brandenburg - Prussia to a kingdom. As soon as Philip V ascended the Spanish throne, Leopold changed his attitude towards Frederick III, and in the so - called crown contract, he gave his consent, that Frederick might assume the title of king.(He called himself, after the coronation at Koenigsberg on the 18th of January, 1701, "Frederick I, king in Prussia). Frederick had, on his turn, to furnish 10 000 auxiliaries to the Emperor.

The chief commanders in the war which was about to be begun now, and which was going to rage for thirteen years, were on the Emperor s side:

Eugene, prince of Savoy, general of the Imperial troops;

The duke of Marlborough (formerly John Churchill), English
        general; and

Leopold, duke of Dessau, Prussian general;

on France 's side:

General Catinat;

The duke of Vendome; and

The elector of Bavaria.

18

Spain, the prize, was of only small importance in this war, as it was carried on chiefly in Italy, the Netherlands and Germany.

The hostilities began in Italy. The French general Catinat had chosen a strong position. Eugene, the commander of the Imperial army, surprised him, however, and Catinat was defeated. The latter's place at the head of the French army was then taken by Villeroi, but he too had to retreat, after he was beaten by Eugene at Chiari, and was moreover taken prisoner. Thereupon France sent considerable reinforcements to Italy, and placed at the head of her army the duke of Vendome, who engaged Eugene seriously for some time.

The situation of the Imperial troops became worse, when Vendome and the elector of Bavaria decided to unite their armies, and to direct them towards Vienna. For this purpose the elector entered the Tyrol, and their plan would doubtlessly have been success - fully carried out but for the brave population of the Tyrol which rose under the leadership of Martin Sterzinger, and compelled the elector to leave the Tyrol. The elector returning to Bavaria de- feated, assisted by Villars, the "Marshal ofFrance", the Imperial troops under Styrum at Hoechstaedt on the 20th of September,1703.

The elector of Bavaria appeared to Eugene now, to be the most formidable of the enemies, and he declared that on behalf of his efficiency, the power of this opponent had to be broken first.

He made therefore arrangements with Marlborough, who occupied the
Spanish Netherlands with an army composed of English and German
troops, for the union of their armies. They met in Bavaria, and
after some smaller engagements with the enemies a decisive battle
was fought at Hoechstaedt - Blenheim, on the 13th of August, 1704.

The united armies of Eugene and Marlborough consisted of
52 000, those of France and the elector of Bavaria of 56 000 men.
At first the French under Tallard and Marsin, and the Franco -
bavarians under the elector were successsful, but towards the end
of the battle they were completely beaten. It was greatly due to
duke Leopold of Dessau and his troops that the battle had taken
such a favorable turn for the Imperial cause. By this victory the
whole south of Germany was lost for the French, and especially the
route to Vienna was blocked. Henceforth France was reduced to
defend herself. The elector of Bavaria, after the battle of Hoch-
staedt fled, and the ban of the Empire met him and his brother,
the archbishop of Cologne.

In the Spanish Netherlands Marlborough had been victorious
throughout, but the Dutch population prevented him from decisive
actions, fearing that they would lose the profitable transit com-
merce to Swede, and the Hanseatic league of Germany.

The Emperor had ceded his pretended rights concerning the
Spanish succession, to his second son archduke Charles in Sept-

He made therefore arrange.ents with Marlborough, who occupied the Spanish Netherlands with an army composed of English and German troops, for the union of their armies. They met in Bavaria, and after some s.aller engagements with the enemies a decisive battle was fought at Hoechstaedt - Blenheim, on the 13th of August, 1704.

The united armies of Eugene and Marlborough consisted of 52 000, those of France and the elector of Bavaria of 56 000 men. At first the French under Tallard and Marsin, and the Franco - bavarians under the elector were successsful, but towards the end of the battle they were completely beaten. It was greatly due to duke Leopold of Dessau and his troops that the battle had taken such a favorable turn for the Imperial cause. By this victory the whole south of Germany was lost for the French, and especially the route to Vienna was blocked. Henceforth France was reduced to defend herself. The elector of Bavaria, after the battle of Hoch- staedt fled, and the ban of the Empire met him and his brother, the archbishop of Cologne.

In the Spanish Netherlands Marlborough had been victorious throughout, but the Dutch population prevented him from decisive actions, fearing that they would lose the profitable transit com- merce to Swede, and the Hanseatic league of Germany.

The Emperor had ceded his pretended rights concerning the Spanish succession, to his second son archduke Charles in Sept-

ember, 1703. In the following spring Charles, assuming the title
"King Charles III", landed, accompanied by an English fleet, at
Lisbon, from where he entered successfully Catalonia, and later
(1706) even for a short time Madrid. The English fleet under
admiral Rooke sailed in the meantime south along the Spanish coast
and occupied Gibraltar in the name of England. Twenty days afterwards a battle was fought between the English and French fleets
off Malaga, which was, however, resultless. The English men-of-
war retreated the following day without being pursued by the
French fleet.

The duke of Savoy prompted his defection from the alliance with
France, because he had just suspicions, that she intended to drive
him out of his own country. French troops held most of the forti-
ied places, when he decided to enter the coalition against Louis X
The French general Vendome had now the double task to punish
Victor Amadeus of Savoy for his unloyalty to the French alliance,
and furthermore to hold in check the Imperial troops under prince
Eugene. To drive the duke of Savoy out of his capital Turin, the
French court sent later La Feuillade with 25 000 men and a great
number of artillery for the siege of that town. Eugene, rein-
forced by several German princes, especially Leopold of Dessau
with his brandenburgians, came to the assistance of Turin. He

defeated La Feuillade, the duke of Orleans and Marsin completely
on the 7th of September, 1706, under the walls of Turin. This
battle was so decisive that the French power in Italy was perfectly broken. Eugene, recognizing this fact, exclaimed after the
battle of Turin: " Italy is ours . " Milan surrendered now too,
and a few weeks afterwards Naples opened its gates to the Imperial
troops under general Daun. The duke of Savoy Victor Amadeus, who
had left Turin during the siege by the French, awaiting the Imperial army in the mountains of the Alps, returned and entered
his capital in a triumphal procession. He also received back all
the places of his country which were previously taken from him by
the French army. Louis, after the disaster of Turin, was compelle
to stipulate the "neutrality of Italy" with the Emperor. Thus the
reign of Philip V was ended in Italy in 1707.

In the Spanish Netherlands the French general Villeroy, acting
with great caution after his defeat at Hoechstaedt, remained
during the year 1705 chiefly in the reserve. Marlborough too
was prevented from decisive actions by the Dutch generals. In
September 1706, however, a battle took place between the two
armies which ended with the defeat of the French, and as a consequence the principal cities of the Netherlands Antwerp, Ostend
and brussels surrendered almost without resistance. Marlborough
took possession of them in the name of "Charles III".

defeated La Feuillade, the duke of Orleans and Marsin completely
on the 7th of September, 1706, under the walls of Turin. This
battle was so decisive that the French power in Italy was perfectly broken. Eugene, reco-gnizing this fact, exclaimed after the
battle of Turin: " Italy is ours . " Milan surrendered now too,
and a few weeks afterwards Naples opened its gates to the Imperial
troops under general Daun. The duke of Savoy Victor Amadeus, who
had left Turin during the siege by the French, awaiting the Imperial army in the mountains of the Alps, returned and entered
his capital in a triumphal procession. He also received back all
the places of his country which were previously taken from him by
the French army. Louis, after the disaster of Turin, was compelle,
to stipulate the "neutrality of Italy" with the Emperor. Thus the
reign of Philip V was ended in Italy in 1707.

In the Spanish Netherlands the French general Villeroy, acting
with great caution after his defeat at Hoechstaedt, remained
during the year 1705 chiefly in the reserve. Marlborough too
was prevented from decisive actions by the Dutch generals. In
September 1706, however, a battle took place between the two
armies which ended with the defeat of the French, and as a consequence the principal cities of the Netherlands Antwerp, Ostend
and brussels surrendered almost without resistance. Marlborough
took possession of them in the name of "Charles III".

The command over the French troops in the Netherlands was now
given to Vendome, and he succeeded in regaining some places
(Ghent, Ypres and Bruges). When Eugene learned this, he rushed
from Italy to Marlborough's assistance, and arrived in the Netherlands before his army. He came just in time to command, together
with Marlborough, in the battle at Oudenarde, on the 11th of July,
1708, where Vendome was perfectly beaten. After Eugene's army had
arrived, Lille, Ghent and Bruges were taken. Thus the reign of
Philip V was also terminated in the Netherlands.

Great calamities were added in the interior of France to those
abroad. Though the country was already perfectly impoverished,
and it had become almost impossible to maintain the armies, com-
merce and industry, and especially agriculture were nearly extingu-
ished by the keen winter of 1708/9. In the province of Ile de
France alone 30 000 persons perished by the cold and the following
famine.

Louis XIV, discouraged by so many disasters, was now inclined
to peace at almost any price; he was ready to cede the Spanish
crown and all its possessions to archduke Charles, except Naples
which Philip would keep. The allies, however, demanded the whole
Spanish monarchy for Charles of Austria, the fortresses at the
frontier of the Netherlands, and furthermore restitution of the
possessions of the Empire according to the treaty of Westphalia.

23

Above all they asked that Louis should drive his grandson Philip V
out of Spain.

What a humiliation for this king, who, on the height of his
glory, had almost thought himself a God, and in his whims had
ordered large territories to be devstated by his armies, conferrin
extreme misery upon thousands of innocent people.

Louis was willing to accept all the other conditions except the
one compelling him to make war against his own grandson.

Thereupon the negotiations were discontinued, and war taken up
again.   In Flandres the French general Villards lost the battle
of Malplaquet, which was more trrible than any of the foregoing,
against Eugene and Marlborough on the 11th of September, 1709.
The French troops fought with great bravery, yet the allied armies
were far superior in number, and well provided while the French
were exhausted and nearly starved.   The defeat at Malplaquet was
therefore almost considered a victory in France.   New peace negotiations followed but with no better result than before. Though
Louis was willing to pay subsidies to the allies to make war
against Philip, and even placed French troups to their disposal,
they insisted that he should dethrone himself his grandson, and
oust him from Spain by his own armies. Louis answered: "Puisqu'il
faut faire la guerre, mieux vaut la faire à mes ennemies qu' à
mes enfants."

24

In the meantime the hostilities continued in Spain. Within six months Philip was going to lose and to regain his kingdom. He was now free from tutelage of his grandfather, but he had lost the support of the French armies too. As soon as the French regiments had left Spain, the Imperial army thought Philip V an easy game. In fact archduke Charles and his generals Starhemberg and Stanhope were sucessful in driving Philip back to Madrid, whence he went with what was left of his army, and with the government to Valladolid. "Charles III" thinking Philip's reign terminated, went straight to Madrid, entering it triumphantly. This gave Philip time to profit of the devotion of the Castilians, and of the great talent of the French general Vendome whom Louis XIV had sent to his assistance, though without troops. The first step undertaken by Vendome was to prevent the union of the Portuguese and Charles' army. As a consequence Charles was compelled to retreat to Toledo, and then towards Saragossa. Starhemberg still held Toledo, but he also had to leave, Stanhope with the English troops forming the rear. Vendome attacked the latter, and defeated them, taking Stanhope prisoner, before the Austrian army could come to their assistance. When Starhemberg arrived at the battle field, he was beaten too, taking his retreat in the dark of the night of the 11th of December, 1710. Thus Philip was master of Spain again. He slept that night on captured colors which Ven-

dome had spread for him on the battle field with these words:
" Je vais vous faire le plus beau lit sur lequel jamais roi ait
couché."

Archduke Charles was now again reduced to the possession of
one single city, Barcelona.

General Vendome who for the great services he had rendered to
the Spaniards and their king, was proclaimed the restorer of the
monarchy, died in Spain in 1712.

Emperor Leopold had died in 1705, and was succeeded by his oldest son Joseph I. This had not caused a change in the Austrian
politics, Joseph continuing the war aginst Philip V with great
zeal. In 1711 Joseph I died too, and the inheritance of Austria
came to Joseph's brother, archduke Charles, who was still maintain
ing his claims on the Spanish crown against Philip V in Spain.
It was furthermore to be expected that the German princes would
elot him German emperor.

In England too the accession of a new monarch had taken place,
and this event was going to prove of no less importance for Louis
XIV as well as for Philip V. After the death of William in 1702,
Anne, second daughter of James II had ascended the throne. Anne
would have terminated England's participation in the Spanish succession war soon after her accession but the public opinion was
for thatwar, and its representative as well asthe head of the Whigs

under whose influence she stood, was the duke of Marlborough, ex-
cellent not only as statesman but also as general. Secretly she
favored, however, the Tories, and towards the end of her reign
she found the courage to break with the Whigs. Lord Bolingbroke,
the leader of the Tories, was charged with the office of the prime
minister, and now negotiations of peace were entered with France
(January 1711). Torcy, then French secretary of State says in
his "Mémoires": "Demander à un ministre de France s'il voulait
traiter, c'était demander un malade attaqué d'une longue maladie
s'il voulait guérir." At the same time the duke of Ormond was
charged with the command of the English troops in the field and
the duke of Marlborough recalled.

The opening of peace negotiations by the queen of England meant
practically the disruption of the Great Alliance. It had besides
become matterless by the accession of archduke Charles to the
Austrian throne. England and Holland had no interest to see the
Spanish and American crowns united which would have meant a
disturbance of the ballance of power in Europe similar to that of
the union of the Spanish and French throne for whose prevention
they had been in war with France and Spain for so many years.
England declared therefore during the secret negotiations, to be
willing to promote peace if a guaranty would be given that the
monarchies of Spain and France would never be represented by the

same monarch. Philip V renounced therefore solemnly the French
crown, and the French princes, on their turn, the Spanish crown.

During the year 1711 the war continued but without any decisive
result. Still Louis XIV feared greatly that the allies might
find means to open their way to Paris. He wrote to his general
Villars: " Si un malheur arrive, écrivez - moi; je ramasserai ce
que je pourrai trouver d'hommes; j'irai à Pérone ou à Saint-Quenti,
périr avec vous ou sauver tout l'Etat."

Meanwhile the preliminaries continued between England and France regarding peace. The part of the negotiations which concerned
these two countries was made public, the articles regarding England's allies, kept secret. When the other countries which were
members of the Great Alliance, learned of an agreement between
England and France, they tried to prevent it. Prince Eugene himself went to London for this purpose, but without result. On the
17th of July, 1712, an armistice of 4 months was arranged between
England and France, according to which England withdrew her
troops.

After the English soldiers had left the battle field, Villars
gained some slight advantages over the allies. This was the open
signal for the dissolution of the Great Alliance. On the 7th of
November, 1712, Portugal concluded an armistice; on the 4th of

28

March, 1713, the duke of Savoy followed. On the 11th of April
peace was signed at Utrecht between Spain and France on one side,
and England, the United Provinces of Holland, Brandenburg and
Savoy on the other side. Two days later Portugal joined the treat
To Philip V was assigned Spain, the Indies, and the extended Spanish possessions in America, to England France's territories at the
Hudson Bay, New Foundland, Nova Scotia and New Brunswick, furthermore the Spanish fortress Gibraltar. Holland gained some commerc-
ial advantages and military securities at the boundary. Prussia
obtained the acknowledgement of the Royal title, and of the
sovereignty over Neuchatel and Valengin. Savoy received Sicily.
France was furthermore compelled to recognize the protestant
dynasty in England to dismiss the pretender James III.

Emperor Charles was offered Milan, Naples and the Spanish Nether
lands. But he, who had hoped so long to become king of Spain, and
to possess all her territories, was not satisfied with such a
small part. He continued therefore the war, together with some
of the states of the empire. Soon, however, he saw, that there
was no hope left for him for a final victory, and he joined the
treaty of Utrecht by the treaty of Rastadt (1714). To the elector
of Bavaria and his brother, the archbishop Joseph Clemens of
Cologne their former possessions were given back.

29

C O N C L U S I O N .

What was the direct outcome of this tremendous war that had been raging from 1701 to 1714, involving almost all states of Europe, and what were its consequences ?

Of the greatest importance was, without doubt, that the Bourbons were successful in repelling the Hapsburgs in Spain. Austria had lost the Spanish crown for ever.

For a moment it had been doubtful whether the Bourbon dynasty was going to settle in Spain. The duke of burgundy, Dauphin of France, had died in February, 1712, of a malignant kind of measles. His wife and five years old son followed him soon in death. There was only left now a weak child of two years of age for the succession in France, and Philip V could have reserved his rights on the French throne, by renouncing the Spanish crown, and contenting himself with the two Sicilies and Piedmont. The only pretender left for Spain would then have been the duke of Savoy. Still Philip resisted the entreaties of his grandfather, and remained king of Spain. In order to exclude the house of Savoy as

much as possible from the Spanish succession Philip arranged moreover a new law according to which women could ascend the throne
only if there was no male descendant either of the direct or a
branchline, born on Spanish territory.

The losses of France have been pointed out above. The worst
consequence of the war for her was, however, the remarkable decrease of her authority in the concert of the European nations.
Louis XIV had had to appeal several times to the mercy of the alli
and it was only natural that France was not considered by them
with the same respect after the Spanish succession war as it had
been before.

The house of Hapsburg had lost the Spanish crown, yet it was
compensated in the Netherlands and Italy.   This was very favorable as Austria could not think of attaching Spain to her crown
after archduke Charles had become king of Austria and emperor of
Germany: the other European countries would not have consented to
it for the reason of maintaining the balance of power.

The kings of Prussia and Savoy had gained considerably by the
war, less in territories than in their position among the Great
Powers. Prussia had territories at all the frontiers of the
German empire, Savoy possessed the two extreme parts of Italy,

and from this period may be counted the evolution which finally ended in the unity of Germany and the unity of Italy.

- - - - - - - - -

Property of
Mitge Brook Library

Milton Keynes UK
Ingram Content Group UK Ltd.
UKHW051923240624
444478UK00004BA/47